Devolution

Caitlin Press Inc.
8100 Alderwood Road,
Halfmoon Bay, BC V0N 1Y1
www.caitlin-press.com

Cover design by Vici Johnstone
Text design by Sarah Corsie
Printed in Canada

Cover image: adapted from "The Collective Invention" by René Magritte, 1934

Excerpt from *Shame* by Salman Rushdie (page 32)
Copyright © 1983 by Salman Rushdie, used by permission of
The Wylie Agency LLC

Caitlin Press Inc. acknowledges financial support from the Government of Canada
and the Canada Council for the Arts, and the Province of British Columbia through
the British Columbia Arts Council and the Book Publisher's Tax Credit.

Library and Archives Canada Cataloguing in Publication
Devolution : poems and fables / Kim Goldberg.
Goldberg, Kim, 1954- author.
Canadiana 20190198826 | ISBN 9781773860268 (softcover)
LCC PS8613.O434 D48 2020 | DDC C811/.6—dc23

DEVOLUTION

POEMS AND FABLES

KIM GOLDBERG

CAITLIN PRESS

Table of Contents

Atlantis

In the lost city of Atlantis, we drift from god
to god. The animals on display
have slipped their feathered cages and
gilt chains. The Big Top sits empty
not even a flea in the matchbox seats.
It was tricky at first, a skid through marbles
on the curve. The swifts departed in ash plumes
rising from the lacerated
rim of our existence. They took the night
with them. We now know through inductive
reasoning and computer simulations
that the swifts were the night.
And with night comes sleep, and with sleep
dreams. You see where this narrative
of privation is leading.

Wait. There, behind the goat-shaped cloud—
I think I see another god.

Deception Pond

At Deception Pond small fish believe they are giants, titans of the deep. When raindrops pelt the surface the fish declare a state of emergency, round up all the caddis fly larvae and charge them with breaking the sky. They detain them in discarded beer cans without benefit of trial or legal representation. Meanwhile, the fish dispatch midges to repair the sky. The fish eat a few midges in front of the others to motivate a diligent work ethic. The midges do an excellent job (although really, the rain has simply stopped). The fish hold a parade in honour of the midges but accidentally devour them in their lust. A marching band of aquatic snails pounds out a beat on timpani of sodden candy bar wrappers. The rhythm triggers a seizure of group fornication. A darkness befalls the pond as the muddy bottom is flicked to the top. When the silt settles, the pond has turned anaerobic. The fish gasp, roll their eyes, heave red gills open and closed like a demon's bellows. They blame this sabotage on the caddis fly larvae, who must have escaped their beer cans. The sun is now bright upon the airless pond. The fish still believe they are titans but must seek cover to regroup. They school into shady water along the edge, unaware it is the shadow of a heron.

Atmospheric Inversion

The best thoughts, the ones that could save us, that could mend all
clouds and reformulate blood-dipped bayonets as blades of
grass, these are the ones that are smuggled out as
contraband flints strapped to the underside of houseflies hell-bent for
liberty… Give me wingtime with no flight plan or give me
carrion luggage…Yet even in their absence, I see stabs of
hope, backlit motes of dreamy possibility paddling upstream on
a wishbone raft, small tufts of unslung idea that somehow ducked false
contentment on the rockpile of the herd mind. The butterflies have
disappeared as sacrificial offerings in the crusade against
gypsy moths. Gone are swallowtails, mourning cloaks, apollos,
from scrubbing the landscape raw with gut-blind ethnic
cleansing. My mind is a white room where a washerwoman stoops
from scrubbing the landscape raw with gut-blind ethnic
gypsy moths. Gone are swallowtails, mourning cloaks, apollos,
disappeared as sacrificial offerings in the crusade against
contentment on the rockpile of the herd mind. The butterflies have
a wishbone raft, small tufts of unslung idea that somehow ducked false
hope, backlit motes of dreamy possibility paddling upstream on
carrion luggage… Yet even in their absence, I see stabs of
liberty… Give me wingtime with no flight plan or give me
contraband flints strapped to the underside of houseflies hell-bent for
grass, these are the ones that are smuggled out as
clouds and reformulate blood-dipped bayonets as blades of
the best thoughts, the ones that could save us, that could mend all.

threes

1.
three men by the corndog cart
take to the sky as crows
their business suits and patent
leather loafers become black
feathers and claw feet
as they loft into the blue
their three briefcases
now dark maws stretched wide
with sound and meteorology
the landlocked people
feel a momentary warm breath of
wing beats as they reach
for the mustard
                    and then nothing

2.
three men in a rowboat
fight over two oars until
they knock a hole in
the floorboards and an octopus
scuttles in   the men
are out-armed but the octopus knows
the destination   the creature rows
all night with two arms
and clasps the three men in an
adhesive embrace with
the other six   by morning
they clear the birth canal
the exhausted octopus deposits
her naked squealing cargo
on the beach

3.
three men in a boardroom
thirty stories high
discuss double-hulled
tankers while erasing small
islands from marine charts
a hiccup in their
hearts leaps from three
throats and bangs its head against
the triple-glazed window
trying to see all thirty
stories at once

Staging

The opera had gone on far too long. The audience came and went as needed for sandwiches, hip replacements, jail sentences. But it was glorious. I composed it myself and was performing it with the koalas, high in the eucalyptus forest. The orchestra smashed metal plates with the ferocity of dueling moon rovers. My lyrics were inscrutable without the universal translator. Yet our harmonies were skeins of silver geese reaching all the way to Cassiopeia's left eye. The finale was perhaps too abrupt. (All the reviewers mentioned this.) When they slid me out of my oven casing on a steel rail, fully baked with golden puff pastry nicely crusted on my torso, I could still taste the sweet warmth of the koalas' eucalyptus breath.

The Old Woman and the Sea

Somewhere beyond silent streets and woodlands
beyond upheaved graveyards, empty schools
dry spillways, vacant
hibernaculums for little brown bats
beyond the last larval foodplant for the last
western tiger swallowtail
an old woman sits by the sea untangling
the nets of each life she can recall
from the Time Before. Her cabin above the tideline
is sparse as birdsong in a northwest
squall. She cooks over a burn barrel beside
her shack, stokes it with driftwood and whatever
tumbles ashore. Once an old door
made a landing, then a desk still intact.
She grills any scrap of flesh
the sea hacks up—bull kelp, moon jellies
three-eyed eels. Eats them with succulent stems
of glasswort growing in the sand.
When evening comes, she flings each newly
sorted net upon the ocean like a bedsheet
for each is a piece of the planetary
genome. She is waiting
for the nets to find one another, reconnect
end-to-end, spiral beneath the waves. Replicate.
But each net returns alone
an enfolded mass of knots, bone
chitinous exoskeletons, bloated elongate bodies
of the unknown.

Animal

A man parted his beard one morning and a bear walked out. It walked down the hall, out the front door, across the street, and all the way to the other end of town, whereupon it consumed a fox terrier tethered to a lamppost outside an ice cream parlour. The terrier's owner came rushing out and hurled her banana split at the bear as it lumbered off toward the tire store. The man arrived on the scene shortly thereafter. He found his bereaved fiancée inspecting the slack leash still tied to the lamppost. She took one look at her husband-to-be and that silly 'd' hanging from his chin (it was a very small 'd') and realized she could never marry a man who had let his bear escape. When their eyes met, he heard a faint thud, as though somewhere a sea star had fallen from the sky, landing in a compost heap.

Devolution

You were sitting on the stars. I didn't notice you
at first. I was skipping the moons of Jupiter across
eternity's black hiss. You sat very still
and in the shadow of a large dog's
last breath. Just smoking a cigarette and watching me
skip moons. Each ripple was the raspy alarm call
of a canyon wren trapped in the geologic
grip of moons becoming stones becoming sand
becoming beach glass becoming a coral reef becoming
bleached muslin as the electrostatic waters recede
exposing single-celled life to the face of
complexity. I liked the grating sound of live wires
unbraiding themselves until the moons
ran out. That's when I turned and saw you
saw the orange tip of your cigarette as you took a
long drag. You flicked it aside and it became
another star.
"Want to see something cherry-bent faraday?" you asked.
"What does that mean?" I said.
"No fun if I tell you. Follow me."
So I did. Past the Shrunken Nebula and the Palace of Historic
Eyebrow Gestures and finally the Swale of Decomposing
Art that no one understood. That's when you showed me
the burial caves deep in your body. You led me
on hands and knees. By the end we had to belly-crawl. When we
reached the Wall of Bells we had become
centipedes out of necessity. The bells were birdcages
housing creatures we couldn't see—flash of feather
a furry arm reaching out from underneath, curling
over brass skirt, golden eyes blinking in dark cavities.
The bells spoke, trying to convince us of something. Their tone
was urgent but I could not grasp the meaning.

They all yammered at once and in a dead
language. Their yearning was a hotplate beneath my
hundred feet. Soon I had one hundred
corn tortillas. I decided to open a taco truck. It was an unmet
niche market in the burial caves gastronomy. You were
watching me again and smoking another cigarette.

Basket Weaver

When ten percent of the population could no longer walk, the old woman wove a large basket from willow branches that were still alive and growing. The basket was covered with narrow green leaves from the living branches. The leaves danced and shimmied in the wind. They flashed in the sun like a bright ball of herring spawning their puny brains out in the tossing surf. The leaves were swooning and copulating like only chlorophyll can—beyond the strictures of blood and bone and moist openings. The basket was the old woman's gift to the town. She told the stricken people to enter one by one, crawling to it on their elbows and bellies since their legs no longer worked. No matter how many people entered, the basket never got full. This went on for quite some while until all the belly-crawlers were inside and the basket had been closed up tight. The people who entered were never seen again, but each night fireflies would sift out through the slits between the willow branches and light up the town.

Welcome to Morphilia

Welcome to Morphilia! Population variable.
Where birds sing out names of bank-robbers
adulterers, corpse-stealers, and each flower
is a secret portal to the clubmoss uprising
(which we don't discuss).

If you want a home cooked mealworm
jambalaya or an irrational slab of
πr^2 , Maybelline's awaits you until the next
remodel occurs. And should your aging
air-cooled bucket of bosons break down
while visiting our postcard-perfect hamlet
inspired by Rockwell and UNICEF cards
just hoof it over to Phil's Garage.

Phil sleeps with the tulip bulbs now
but someone in coveralls can order your parts
which will never arrive because
come every night the voracious earth
devours itself and extrudes new shapes—cafés
people, flowers, garages, mathematical
equations, botanical revolutions
you and the sputtering tin yuletide
you rode in on, bank-robbers, corpse-stealers
sinners of every star and stripe
(as well as the innocent to preserve
the Hegelian dialectic).

Only the birds remain since they are not tethered
to much of anything and are rumoured to be
some sort of remote surveillance device.

Charm

A charm of goldfinches flew
from the smokestack of an abandoned factory
at the edge of town. It was more of an explosion really
a bursting forth of sound and feather and soot.
Enshrouded in coal dust and creosote
the charm soared above streets and was widely
misread as a murmuration of starlings—those pestilent
inkpots on wings. Boys ran for their slingshots
having already learned a certain hierarchy
of being. And when the fallen were inspected
the townsfolk could clearly see the citrus yellow
feathers beneath the smudge. A decision was made
to confiscate all slingshots because no one
could judge the long-term consequences of slaughtering
a charm. Hearts fluttered

behind breastbones. The town clock froze.
Residents returned to their homes,
brought dogs inside, locked doors, lit candles
in teacups, pulled old books down from
shelves and sat in darkness by windows
clutching their books for comfort, for memories
of what things meant, for defence
against whatever may enter.

Caught Between the Devil

I was caught between the devil and your deep blue
seedpod with one foot in the gravitational
field of dreams basting that crooked stitch in twine that saved
the whole nine yards of raw milk once I found your needle-
nose pliers in the playshack. I worked my fingers to the
phone trying to dial your bumbershoot in the dark
night of the chip bowl. Yet we both know that many hands make
light bulbs work, so what I really need here is a good kick in the
pantheon of gods and godlets. But they are all busy out
back in the woodshed pissing up a rope long enough
to hang themselves. And even though you never answered
my trick or entreaty, I suspect you heard it through the
grey time from your perch in the attic where you were
eating like a bird in the handkerchief, which we're
told is worth two live births over my dead body
of evidence that has grown colder than a witch's
titular status as chief herbalist and dingbat roaster. They said
you were under the weatherman. But aren't we all really,
when it comes right down to it? Who among us stands
tall in the saddle (or shadow) of forecasting (or
flycasting)? There but for the grace of sod
go my certified organic rutabagas. Buddy can you spare
some global climate change? Standing in saddles is
unsafe saxophone practice to begin with, and I know deep
down in my kumquat that you're smarter than that
(although you can also be a gigantic pain in the
assembly wharf when you want to, like now). The problem
with life in the doghouse is that you can't sweep the
blueberry crumble from the master's table under the
rug rats (why did we never have chili peppers?)
because they flew the coupon
to the moon.

Rabbits

One morning the landscape got up and walked away. The rabbits were the first to notice. No grass to flirt in, no earth to tunnel, no gardens to decimate. Each rabbit gazed at its colleagues suspended in empty space. There was still an abundance of sky. But the horizon was as vague as a pointillist painting, having no terrain to conjoin. No union of heaven and earth, as the Daoists would say. With more free time on their paws, the rabbits spent much of it copulating. There was little else to occupy them. When the other species took measure of their collective situation and the impact of rampant rabbit fornication, the Animal Kingdom passed anti-copulation laws (which were really anti-rabbit laws because the other species knew how to keep their privates private or read a book or resort to auto-erotic techniques if need be). The rabbits soon had enough progeny of voting age to repeal the anti-copulation laws and enact new laws mandating the construction of sexual amusement parks in every town. There were no raw materials with which to build these amusement parks or towns. So these items remained mental constructs until enough creatures had passed away from starvation that their bones could be used for scaffolding and their hides for tent canvas, awnings, slides, water beds, camel cabanas and many other applications. Rabbit hedonism ensued for quite some while, with the other species sulking in the bleachers. Until one day, under a blue sky adrift in tufted clouds, a new landscape arrived seemingly out of nowhere. Much coitus interruptus occurred. The other species cheered and scurried to anchor themselves to the earth. This caused the new landscape (which was really an old and arthritic landscape that had been on the road too long) to drop dead from a heart attack. No one noticed.

Curtain Call

When the full moon falls from the sky
and the world goes dark, we do not see
the heron built from car parts lift off
from its display by the hot dog wagon to impale
the bright moon on its crankshaft bill, causing
the moon to deflate as the light seeps out,
or the ship made of twigs that sets sail
and catches the dishrag moon in its loose-knit
bow, or the wooden crab the size of a
Guernsey cow that seizes the blackness to scrabble
toward the crab dock and release the convicts
in the traps beneath, or the havoc this wreaks
for nearby condominiums, which quickly fill up
with crustaceans on the lam, or the consequences
this will have on world banking and interest rates
as the mortgage-paying population is increasingly
displaced onto the streets by arthropods who like
dry martinis and big screen TV. As we pull
our sleeping bags tighter in our sandy beds
beneath the highway next to the sewer outfall,
we will never suspect that public art
was the cause. We will simply, in our ignorance
and superstition and aching need to find
a larger organizing principle at work in the Universe,
tell ourselves the gods were against us, we had
a good run, it's time to kill the babies
and let the audience go home.

Arrival

A land where wolves did howl 'til dawn
Where muskrats wove each home from reeds
I don't know why the bees have gone
Have never heard a wolf at dawn
The beaver's tail does sound alarm
No squash will grow from last year's seeds
On land where wheels now howl 'til dawn
And townhomes rise where once stood reeds

Special Collection

And we know this is a library by the mastodon columns bracketing our under
standing, their slow forage, the greying text of stony hide

by the flow of ideas in and out, tidal washing our soiled brain, our shared
pathways wired tight with twisted tines from aborted shopping carts and
clingfasts of green slime

by the storytime creekbed hissing getaway plans, popping bubblegum lips,
blowing mud kisses to overflying crows

by the ceaseless thrum of fluorescent traffic above

by the pigeon-suited pinkertons strutting the upper gallery (ever vigilant for
pocketed words, sedition in a herd of bottle caps)

by the roomful of silent readers, gravity-slouched beneath the weight of our
narrative equations, seated on loosened capstones, exhibiting the shallow-
breath'd torpor that descends upon a population leaf-pressed in life's gaunt
novella

by the special collection slumbering behind the archival wall, swaddled in
salvation army gossamer, the white gloves we must don so not to damage them
with our clumsy eggbeater minds, our wide-slot toaster eyes

Stairway to Nowhere

The moment we saw the Stairway to Nowhere in *Town and Country* magazine, we knew we had to have one of our own. We searched the New England countryside until we found the perfect eighteenth-century cottage in Francestown. It was practically a twin to the magazine cottage. We tried to barter with the owner, offering him a silk-moth farm, then a herd of giraffes we had acquired last year in Kenya. But he was firm on his asking price of five bottled sunsets. And we were wetting ourselves for the stairway, so we caved.

Demolishing the top of the colonial staircase (along with the top floor of the cottage) went faster than anticipated once we enlisted Barton's Stampede Renovations. The hoof marks enhanced the distressed appeal of the wide-plank pumpkin pine floorboards. We spent the next eight months decorating the now roofless walls and rooms with antique hay-saws and baby carriage wheels and yellowing bridal gowns scavenged from antique stores and abandoned churches. We practically popped when we found a stuffed beaver and porcupine and a moose antler candelabrum in a taxidermy shop that had been foreclosed on.

At the top of the Stairway to Nowhere we built a small platform from cottonwood fluff so we could sit in a dugout canoe and sip our aged apple brandy while renaming the constellations overhead. We debated about when to call *Town and Country*. We should send them pictures first. The viewing platform was our own embellishment—a detail not found in the original magazine photo since the top of the page had been torn out by a previous reader who wanted a recipe on the other side. We then began to ponder whether the original stairway in the magazine might have led somewhere after all. Perhaps to a second floor of the house. No matter! That makes our redecoration truly original. We will wow the *Town and Country* editors and design mavens with our radical vision that melds antebellum history with the contemporary decolonial thrust of a post-modern cultural ethos while simultaneously deconstructing the contrived barrier cleaving nature from humanity. With that, we downed our brandies.

That night, from our four-poster moss-trimmed beetle bed, we watched the silhouette of foxes padding up and down the stairway. A shooting star burned across the sky.

When spiders dream

Truth is just a constellation
pinpricks yearn for mind's frail join
we're shooting stars inside a barrel
stump remains when tree is gone

pinpricks yearn for mind's frail join
come view the legless refugees
stump remains when tree is gone
send sacred cows to plough the field

come view the legless refugees
waiting, swelling, keening, lasting
send sacred cows to plough the field
stickpin our hopes to spent messiahs

waiting, swelling, keening, lasting
what happens when the stars fall out
stickpin our hopes to spent messiahs
then build more telescopes to watch

what happens when the stars fall out
we pity penguins fouled with warmth
then build more telescopes to watch
how spiders burn their tapestries

we pity penguins fouled with warmth
for distance makes the eye grow sharp
how spiders burn their tapestries
while vastness shrinks the pixel count

for distance makes the eye grow sharp
and tree trunks stand till axe cleaves bark
while vastness shrinks the pixel count
let's leave the universe ajar

and tree trunks stand till axe cleaves bark
we're shooting stars inside a barrel
let's leave the universe ajar
Truth is just a constellation

Opening Act

We are sitting in a darkened theatre waiting for the play to begin. It is a full house. The entire run is sold out. The squeak of a pulley tells us the curtain has opened. But we do not see this because there are no stage lights, just blackness. Is the lighting operator asleep? Drunk? Murdered? Run off with the cashier? We hear movement, actors pacing, props being shoved around. Something falls, breaks. A vase maybe? A skull? No words are spoken, just the occasional grunt. We assume it is human but cannot be sure. This must all be part of the script, this darkness, this enigma, some avant-garde theatre experiment. We are game. We roll with it. To flee to the well-lit lobby for safety would be an act of cultural illiteracy. Patrons begin to murmur to their partners. I reach out to touch your arm but there is only sand. A gull cries. I smell brine.

autumn breeze

life   expectancy   always   fails
   like   eiderdown   after   frost
     lost   entrails   along   freeways
  leftleaning   eyes   analyze   fur
    ligament   eternal   afterlife   for
      lumpenkind   every   answer   forges
   likely   extinction   anomalous   findings
leap   everywhichway   asknotwhatyourcountrycando   foryou
      lovers   entwined   anger   forgotten
     lets   eat   a   fondue
    lets   erect   a   freakingshelfunit
   lets   enter   another   frequency
lodestars   ebb   and   flow
  leaving   existential   anthems   for
     leviathans   ephemeral   as   firebombs
   lodging   eventually   above   federalreservevaults
leading   everbelieving   acolytes   farther
   leeward   ending   another   freewheeling
    lesson   editorializing   again   ferfucksake
  leaves   escape   at   fall
like   erudite   anachronisms   finding
   little   enlightenment   afterall   feels
     like   entering   apogee   forever

cake

lost in an alley we sought our gods
stowed our bundt pans in gravel burrows
sweet keepsakes from an earlier epoch
tossed in an alley we caught our gods
shifting numbers to hide the curvature of thought
when the bubble burst the moths turned gold
but we lost the alley defrauded by gods
who stowed our bundt pans in gravel burrows

35 years

for Chelsea Manning

Who does not know
the meaning of the mouth
sewn shut,
of two crows impaled
upon the gatepost?

> They say Jesus
> was a hermaphrodite—early
> medieval art depicts him
> as a woman complete
> with tiny breasts

There are things
that cannot be said. No—
it's more than that:
there are things that cannot
be permitted to be true

> Before the Church erupted
> and burst wide
> its rugged seed, the two-spirited ones
> were honoured as healers
> and seers

We carried the special being
in a golden litter
borne on poles atop
our shoulders (I saw this
in a Fellini film)

Traitor or soothsayer—
quantum physics tells us
it's all relative
and position-
dependent

Two halves make a hole
where the rain gets in
and the truth leaks out
and starts my mind a-wondering
where bullets go

Zeno's paradox
protects each drone operator
shields his tender nib
of conscience from the button's
bruise—no bomb ever truly arrives

Those who know
do not speak, those who speak
do not know
a bramble crown
awaits them

She gave the world a video
from the cockpit of an Apache
helicopter: American troops
cut down civilians in New Baghdad
laugh

Those church bells tolling
in the distance
are really the sound of war logs
being pounded into a cross
on a hilltop in Kansas

Binary Slippage

Beyond the coal slagheap at the estuary lies an abandoned foundry. Its roofless innards now populated by a young forest of alder and fir climbing above broken walls. I enter through the main door (long gone). For it is here, at the epicentre of nature's repossession of her flesh from the gears, that I have decided to bury my two amygdalae.

I dig a shallow grave, roll my motionless amygdalae into place, cover them beneath a pile of fir cones, old hubcaps, and a desiccated squirrel carcass (which adds just the right touch of recursiveness). My amygdalae are still breathing softly, fogging the pocket mirror I hold near their membraned surface before loading on the cones and tin.

I do not have time to bury them deeper. The blueprint for burial is fading too quickly. I fear I will be left with a shovel, a half-dug hole, my feral neural pathways cackle-dancing in the headlights, and no procedural strand to bind the three.

By the time I finish, the headlights have drained the battery. I must find another way home. Setting out on foot, I discover a message written in the sand by the phainopeplas with their silky black wing tips. (Several months must have elapsed, for I am no longer beside the Nanaimo River estuary but in the California desert near Agua Caliente.) The tiny ridges in the sand, which would have been imperceptible under the sun's harsh glare, form a fine cursive script in the moonlight. This is where I learn that my increasingly drafty mind, distinguished more by vacancies now than furnishings, is just a flimsy stand-in, some cheap simulacrum of an iPad.

My malformed memories, the phainopeplas tell me, are just clumsy metaphors longing for intercourse with other twisted semantic fragments as they grope across a wasteland littered in peptides and machine code. My amnesia, it turns out, is species-wide. The whole of human thought uploaded to the skies— externalized for our transactive benefit, the phainopeplas reassure.

Thank god! At least it isn't *me*. I am just some runty twig spinning in the tumble of techno-cultural contexts beyond my control, misted now by the approaching falls. A rainbow appears in the final moments, defying laws of night and Newtonian physics. This is when I notice the genius of our collective emptying, of our headlong plunge into dark whirlpools of ones and zeros.

Somewhere a Creature

Upon the planet's stony hide unloved
Where sandstorms scour bones to piles of chalk
A kaleidoscopic rash of domes erupts
Passing sense orbs swivel, rumble, gawk

Each hemisphere a mystery inside
Bauble, beast, arcane chemistry?
To look would alter flow of sun and tide
The world's awobble with uncertainty

Beside one dome a garden grows abundant
Beside another knives do claim some flesh
There's talk of secret springs, an end to hunger
Somewhere a creature slips its master's leash

Once the drift toward meaning has begun
It is a thing can never be undone

A tall girl

A tall girl with long, tanned arms wanders the beach at low tide. She is wearing a loose, sleeveless dress the colour of the sky overhead. Her footprints in the wet sand stretch out behind her, comingling with shells, stones, a stray feather, bits of coloured glass buffed smooth as pebbles. The beach ahead is a blank sheet devoid of all impressions and castaways. At her hip hangs a large satchel woven from grass. The satchel's strap is slung diagonally across her lank body. As she walks, she reaches into the bag, retrieving shells, stones, a stray feather, bits of coloured glass buffed smooth as pebbles, and strews them upon the beach. Next she brings out a cool breeze and lets it go. Her loose dress begins to billow.

Sacrament

We are brushing each other's hair
beside the fire. The crackle-pop of trash
and old pallets masks the sound of snapping
twigs (or tiny bones?) in the dark
cytoplasm that surrounds us. Unseen animals
screech, wail, leap from precipices
in the ether. We are a bright nucleus
of stellar gases amid this universe of pissed-on
mattresses and walls that turn to doors
in the blackness. You stop to pick lice from
my scalp, casually eat them—an ancient
reflex spurred by flame, fear, the lustless
need to connect. I am disgusted,
scramble to my feet, stagger back into the shadow
screaming you're too fried
to keep your shit together, you can't even
brush my hair right, you've ruined everything again!
But all I hear

are wing beats. My words take flight
as small brown bats lofting
from my mouth, gushering into
penumbra, assailing doomed bugs,
echolocating beyond our range. Their existence
known only by secondary evidence:
the slight shifts in air pressure, wisp of
breath on my face, the strobing of your startled eyes
as each bat passes.

Spawn

Under the bluest sky of the year, I stood at the edge of my world
and watched the flickerflashing churn of brimming life, the sea gone
white with sperm—the stench and smoky spew
of diesel-powered winches winding in their nets, beating
out the fish. I watched the shooting stars cascade into
the darkened hold to be later stripped of roe for
Japanese markets. The yawning emptiness between electrons
in the salty air—packed tight today with sirens' wail
and squaggling song from four thousand gulls and brant
aloft beyond the endless snowy drift of milt
whipped thick and scattered into bands of froth along a tideline
with no vanishing point at all.
All of this on the same day that the radioactive cloud
from Japan's nuclear disaster was scheduled to reach our shore—
all of us together in this self-made retroactive cloud
with no vanishing point at all.
We tipped and scattered clamshells in the froth, our lifeline .
lost beyond the endless rift cleaving molten
rock and magma from four thousand songs and plants.
The salty air packed tight today with sirens' wail
in Japanese markets, while the yawning emptiness of our elections
echoes in a darkened hold to be later stripped and sold
as fish bait. We watched the shooting stars cascade into
a diesel-flowered meadow binding all our heads, beating
while it burned until the stench and smoky spew
was traded for the flickerflash of atomic churn. And the sea was gone
under the bluest sky of the year, as we stood at the edge of our world.

Escape from Cyberia

There were wild horses. And a beach. And a storm, I think. No, wait—that's the cover photo on Susan Musgrave's timeline. Maybe there were only some big waves the size of tiny houses on wheels, rolling into shore like a sustainably designed refugee camp, each with an innocent Syrian family inside just trying to survive the civil war at Christmas time, desperately awaiting tins of plum pudding from overseas that would never arrive because Indiegogo froze the plum pudding campaign (which had broken all crowdsourcing records in its first twenty-four hours) after the word 'dessert' was red-flagged by the US State Department's poorly programmed algorithm searching for long-tail keywords—in this case 'desert' since that can signify a variety of potentially terrorist activities, as can 'Bactrian' or 'bivouac' or 'Babel'. All the tiny doors of the tiny houses flew open as soon as the tiny wheels stalled in deep sand, and the Syrian families were tossed out onto the desert on tiny tidal waves of urchins and sea stars and ling cod. The families became wild horses stampeding down the beach to escape the long-tail keywords pursuing them. (Everyone knows horses are afraid of long-tail keywords.) The sharp report of their hooves sounded like machine gun fire, but this was most likely due to the State Department's residual power of suggestion, so I urge you to rise above it as I have tried to. And from our arisen position, we can now see that the horses are not running down a beach or a desert or a sandlot of any sort but rather the hard ceramic tiles of Woodgrove Mall, parting the red and green seas of Christmas shoppers (as Moses himself did) to expose the International Food Court for the CIA mind-control front that it is: a deep-fried spicy Szechuan offshoot of MKUltra.

I am crouched beneath the battery spin-rack in the Everything for a Dollar Store, surreptitiously photographing the entire Food Court spectacle through the window. I am sitting on absolute fucking gold here. No one but me has this story. This could be my comeback.

small birds

small birds, invisible
to distant eye, cry out at dusk
or is it just
the groan of fir limbs
rushed with wind, blown into
each other by forces of covert animation
beyond their control?
a cone drops
lands with soft thud on
forest duff   there is a moment
of stillness in which vectors
pause

      anything is possible

and then a sylvan committee is struck
to determine why the cone
was not more firmly attached
and whether this pattern could
spread to other cones
causing a wide-scale cone drop and crisis
of confidence in forests overall
and are the invisible
birds at fault? their cries
(or errant wind) must be diminished
so the innocent do not become
buried under fir needles and leaf mould
and bat shit, for it is the lofty cones
we care about here, in case
you've lost track
their vital seed will spawn
the next forest
birds come and go
like the wind

Temporary Exhibit

It's been raining for days, thrumming on tin roofs of boatsheds at the abandoned yacht club. Hollow condominium towers loom in the fog, their dark compound eyes staring out to sea. Toyotas and BMWs with doors flung wide sit stalled at traffic lights that still change—all stereos, alloy wheels and other redeemables intact. Only the homeless slumbering in their concrete mausoleum beneath the highway survived the accidental discharge of Belltone's protoype Sonic EM Depopulator, on display for the month at the town's new science museum. Several black bears hibernating in earthen dens up Mount Benson also made it through along with western painted turtles buried deep in the mud at Buttertubs Marsh. And the rough-skinned newts in Bowen Park prevailed. Their orange and brown bodies were pressed snug between rotting logs and soft carpet of wet leaves cladding the forest floor, affording considerable shock absorption.

Hell-n-Back Herb exits the concrete underpass and clatters his shopping cart along the ghostly seawall promenade to Thrifty's. Rain streams from his beaded beard. Not even a shithawk perched on the gunwales of fishboats slapping against the dock. Thrifty's is as forsaken as a coma patient in a persistent vegetative state. Tonight Herb and the crew will feast on Hearty Boy beef stew with French wine and marinated artichoke hearts.

Twilight on Esplanade Street

Roll me the curled lip of chainlink, the ragged kerf
of metal fang on flattened psyche
scraping under. Play me the singsong

down-staircase of white-crowned sparrow flinging last hope
off creosoted hydro pole. Weight me with peeled
logs strapped to flatcars

travelling nowhere—lifeless old bones. The memory
of falling, rolling. Coming undone.
Shush me corroded secrets of steel rails

laid one hundred and fifty years past by men
from China handed numbers for payroll names, plaques,
company epitaphs. Lend me the bent backs

of cottonwoods sighing above me, this doomed escape
from gravity as their strewed tuftings loft 'round
my ankles then settle back to their gravelly

tombs. Read me the smear of gone graffiti
on stop sign. Erasure of someone's 'Home Sweat Home'—
the loss of history. Of her story, the crack pipe,

the bad john, the pocketknife, the salmon-gutting.
Glimpse me the Gabriola ferry chugging across the channel
through slit of grey light pinched

tight between black sausage links gorged with liquified
petroleum gas stamped
PROCOR PROCOR PROCOR PROCOR

not odorized
Strew me committees of cast-off life
abandoned in long grass. The detritus of passion burst,

passed, slowly reabsorbed by this
amoeboid roadside—the greasy McDonald's wrappers,
hot-boxed butts, pull tabs, limp

comet tails of depleted condoms. Take me beyond
the mote of oozing sludge and
bramble rampart to that gauze of white

clover floating between the tracks, pinkening
now with ripeness as the day's boundaries collapse and the sky floods
its alchemical tinctures across forgotten scripts, percolating

whispers of vanished bivalves, a recollection
of sea gooseberries before they fell from their constellations,
this darkening stain

of migratory geese ripping at the seams,
tasting commas, apostrophes, all the salty follicular
wildness of languages left behind.

Broken

The ocean broke
We called a repairman
The sea stars shot hoops using the anemones
We retweeted headlines of planetary collapse
The crows vanished among oily barnacles on the beach
We joined #TeamFollowBack
We waited for miracles
The nudibranchs armed themselves to protect their spots
(The octopi were already well armed)
We grew bored
A relief team arrived to relieve our boredom
We were still bored
We wondered where that blasted repairman was
We called his office
A disembodied voice told us he was already on site
We asked if we could pay in sand dollars
That will cost us an extra fifty push-ups, the voice said
We got the gumboot chitons to do our push-ups for us
(They didn't have as far to push)
The flounder floundered
The sole departed
The tuna tuned up their ukuleles and began to play
The ukuleles had minds of their own—and genitalia
Things were getting out of hand
We still couldn't find the repairman
The ocean was clearly still broken
We asked for a refund
We were told our 30-day guarantee had expired
We launched a Kickstarter campaign to hire a new repairman
We offered moon jellies for perks

We exceeded our stretch goal
Then the first repairman showed up in a bitumen raincoat
He had been working beneath the ocean the whole time
He told us we need a new ocean
Or we could convert to desert with a government rebate

Travelling Man

The Travelling Man rolled into town in his painted-up wagon pulled by two stout fir trees. Yes, you and I know that trees are sessile and cannot pull a peanut, let alone a 900-pound caravan, across the landscape. It must be some sort of trick. And indeed it was. The Travelling Man's engineers had laid a concealed metal track four inches beneath the earth along the main wagon road joining all the towns. At each end of the track, a steam-powered winch was hidden in a hen house. The engineers had worked away night after night with sound-deadening Teflon shovels while the townsfolk slept. The lips of the incision in the earth pressed themselves together like a kiss. They parted only briefly when the tree-platform's wheels slid through on the sunken rails.

The sight of a wagon pulled by fir trees filled the townsfolk with awe. Hearts quickened. Jaws gaped. They had heard rumours, but who could believe? "Anyone who can harness the stasis of forests to get some useful work out of the damn things… Hell's bells! Let's see what else he's got on board!" (This reaction had been predicted by the Travelling Man's market research team, who had been required to sign non-disclosure agreements.)

He stopped his wagon in the middle of Main Street. The town's children raced in from all corners. Their porcelain skulls, thin as wasp nests, bobbed on C1 vertebrae like bright buds beneath their shiny skin and hair.

"Will it bite me?" asked a freckle-faced girl as she reached out to stroke the tree's craggy bark. (Trees of such magnitude had not been seen 'round these parts for quite some while.)

"Course it won't bite you, darlin'! Trees don't bite," laughed the Travelling Man, who had donned his gleaming prosthetic smile at the outskirts of town to hide his teeth, blackened from years of betel-chewing.

The townsfolk followed their children, crowding around the caravan. Brilliantly coloured long-tailed birds were painted on the doors on one side. With a flourish and a piano chord from somewhere, The Travelling

Man swung open the doors to show off his wares. "Plenty for everyone!" he announced.

Gasps rippled through the crowd as the townsfolk marvelled at what they saw (although they understood none of it). They each held out cupped hands to receive their gift. For that was the genius part—the Travelling Man's miracles were free. The blacksmith went away with a small cough. His neighbour took home an arrhythmia. The freckle-faced girl was given a shadow no bigger than a quail egg on her brain.

Closed Circuit

The author at her computer. The author at her computer writing a book. The author at her computer writing a book about people sickened. The author at her computer writing a book about people sickened by their computers. And by their computers' extended families of noisy microwave relatives, relatives who snort and fart and belly up to the blood trough to feed. Relatives who scrape the neural sheathing from each axon and use the shreds to floss their dingy teeth. Relatives who bore into brain casings like teredo worms into a ship's hull. Relatives who copulate shamelessly in city parks and streets and elementary schools to breed more relatives, who shamelessly copulate and snort and fart and belly up and scrape and bore. And copulate some more. Relatives who take up landscape painting, but only so they may paint deserts. Relatives who erect their life-size arid vistas in a three-dimensional art installation around the author, rendering her into a figurine in a diorama. A diorama of the author at her computer. The author at her computer writing a book. The author at her computer writing a book about people sickened. The author at her computer writing a book about people sickened by their computers. The author whose lips and face are scorched without stepping off-set. The author whose eyelids have been taped open under the desert sun for three days. The author whose ears are packed with the ringing of phainopeplas flitting from cactus to mesquite. The author whose fingers are puffed and red from rattlesnake venom. The author whose brain is as soft as porridge perking on a camp stove. The author whose thirst cannot be slaked no matter how many times she plunges her seared face into the palm-lined oasis. The author who goes to bed but cannot sleep in the land where the sun never sets. The author whose pineal gland has been flattened and gut-splattered by an 18-wheeler ripping along a Sonoran desert highway. The author who has a waking dream about an author at her computer, an author writing a book, an author writing a book about people sickened by their computers, an author whose tongue is a burning emergency flare that ignites the sky.

Constant Comment

The hobo in my teacup shakes his fist and shouts at me every morning as I pour the boiling water in. He takes cover behind the teabag then makes it his life raft as the rising sea lofts him to the top, blathering all the way. Last week I thought I heard him yell "climate change." Other times, names of dead presidents, Shakespeare's missing sonnets, a recipe for baked halibut. My therapist says these are projections of my Inner Dialogue with my Angry Fractal Self. Yet the halibut was divine. I embark on a journey to the Golden Fridge over a tricky path of loose hypotheses above the treeline. Even my burro protests. When I return with the milk, the hobo is gone like a mob of pigeons. Ceasing to exist when each bird bursts off in a new direction.

Urban Getaway

The City was tired
> like a man on death row or a newborn foal—tired of waiting, of being
> legless, nameless, tongue-scraped by alien forces.

The City wanted to start over
> strike out, see the world, be roseate spoonbills scissoring dark lagoons,
> taste donkeys gone to market along the ravelling hem of the Sahara, know
> the difference between past and present tense.

The City consulted the stars
> It brought out elderly bronze tools hidden in refugee camps of broken
> pencils by the duck pond. It spent several centuries calculating tangents
> and cosines and parabolic arcs, working like a cookstove or a clawfoot tub
> —sleepless, hair-mussed, thirsty for hope. When the formula was complete,

The City whispered the internal secrets
> to all its constituent parts. The secrets were spider fists acquiring tiny
> targets, hissing softly in meteorological code that if overheard by invading
> soldiers would be mistaken for impending snowfall.

The City let the plan unspool
> like a slack gut of stagnant water crawling out to sea in search of birth
> mother. We leave tonight,

The City gassed off
> when they are sleeping. There will be no room for supplies or provisions
> of any kind—no rucksacks, coleman lanterns, stolen kisses, pup tents,
> touchstones, quantum entanglements. Not even your potholes or condom
> hollows or other vacant spaces. We must all walk out naked, lighter than
> hydrogen, or we will never get away. The parts shivered, shot furtive
> glances, nodded like cars backfiring, street-cleaners whisking cold curbs,
> hot grease singing in swollen dumpsters. No discussion was needed. When
> the sun went down, the boundaries blurred and

The City drifted to the ledge

      shepherding its soundless parts, obedient as a shorn herd of silicon chips
      or a flock of rebar encased in blind faith. Or maybe cheez whiz. One by
      one each canon-balled into the chasm—chin tucked, shoulders hunched,
      knees clasped to sunken chest, rusty testicles plunging headlong, expelling
      last breath in a smudge of confusion, just a small parting gift to the
      occupying troops.

And The City was never seen again

      although on sunny days, vague clusters of miasma leave fuzzy shadows on
      the footprint of the former site. Rumour has it

The City may have reformulated itself into white dwarfs and red giants in the
      winter skies, which astrophysicists now know are actually reflections of
      glistening fish guts wrapped tight as shrunken cowhide at the centre of the
      earth.

Walking Home

Where magic leans across the path
And cottonwoods form green arcade
I enter with my parts in half
Where magic leans across the path
Bushtits weave each silver strand
To darn the pieces into lace
Where magic leans across the path
And cottonwoods form green arcade

Field Work

Daily she waited for the afternoon rains to bring her a new species. She had managed to craft a few trees from the leftover mud and sticks and moss and stumps. On the day it rained fish, she collected them in large baskets and rolled them to the sea. When it rained frogs, she filled satchel after satchel and carried them to ponds and streams.

The day of the bird and butterfly downpour was unfortunate. So many wings sheared off in the descent. She worked all night mending. In some cases, she had to reattach wings from the smallest birds to bodies of the largest butterflies. She placed each repair on a leaf bed in a large crate and wheeled them out to a meadow the next morning for release.

All that was left to repopulate were the vacant savannas of asphalt and fractured juttings of glass and steel. Nothing that had rained down so far would survive in this zone. But then the rats fell from the sky, complete with their fleas. Using a large piece of ripe goat cheese as a lure (the goats had rained down earlier), she led the rats en masse across the hills to a clearing of bituminous rubble. The rats sheeted across the hillside in an undulating blanket of scabby fur until they reached the edge of the steel-and-tar-pocked terrain, whereupon they broke into a million pieces, each scuttling into its own dark crevice to meditate upon the comparative densities of muscle and bone.

On her way back across the hills, she wondered if this particular installation, the rats, had been wise. As creatrix she did have some discretionary power. But how can anyone forecast the complex web of cause and effect? Let alone a mere Divinity & Reclamation student from Andromeda U completing her PhD thesis.

a brief history of paradise

left behind:

a finnish sculpture garden filled with human
teeth—the enigma of these ten thousand
tiny glint-suns in earthen mouths, all the bundle-nests
of pregnant squirrels catch fire

elsewhere in the northern hemisphere:

on a street in drain oregon
a wall melts beside arlene's where coffee is still
five cents and the grill-boy fries sows ears all day
lord sandwich demanded his meat
between bread slabs so he never had to leave
the gambling table

history hiccups along:

a captain is consumed on sandwich islands
(more pot roast than sandwich) thus ending his discoveries
of not so new land masses
ten thousand solar flares enamel-bright flash
beneath coconut palms while
masticating the good captain's musculature
sculpting a preordained narrative of
conquest and
                        paradox
ebb and
            flotation devices atwirl

in the blossom sway of the sun-infested garden

Ground Path

Gently, gently, at first I was afraid of wasps by day and slugs by night—
the wet kiss of soft flesh spread wide in long grass. My slow hunt for wasps by
day and slugs by night in this world gone wild beyond the breakers.

In long grass, my slow hunt for a life without shoes, cellphones, wifi. The
world's gone wild beyond the breakers in my basement. I am safe down here
in a life without shoes, cellphones, wifi. I count microwatts to fall asleep each
night in my basement.

I am safe down here but I can't remember the reason I count microwatts
to fall asleep each night as I thread my dreamy path into the planet. I can't
remember the reason we stitched our lives with frequencies as I thread my
dreamy path into the planet and tie the knot with my bare feet. We stitched
our lives with frequencies—the wet kiss of soft flesh spread wide as you tie
my knot with your bare feet. Gently, gently. At first I was afraid.

Loves and Fishes

A salmon walks into a fishing derby and says "Give me a two-seater."

"Why, mister?" asks the attendant renting out kayaks from a kiosk in the park. "There's only one of you. A two-seater will cost you more."

"Never you mind, sonny boy," says the salmon. (Salmon talk like this for some reason.) "Just give me a two-seater."

The salmon gets his two-seater and carries it down the bank to launch it at the mouth of the Millstone River in downtown Nanaimo. As he slides the kayak into the sea, he notices a few humans underwater, tethered to the shore, their smooth bodies swaying back and forth.

"Hmmph! I can do better than those puny things," he grunts. And he starts paddling toward the cluster of kayaks bunched further out.

"Hey, slow it down, buddy!" another salmon shouts. "We got lines in the water here."

At just that moment, a human shoots out of the water straight up in the sky, arcing its sleek body like a comma suspended in mid-air for a single gravity-defying moment until a salmon begins to reel it in. The human thrashes this way and that but is no match for the laws of physics or fabulist fiction.

"*That* little thing?" our salmon says to himself as he sets a new tack away from the group.

"Stay within the marked boundary, sir!" blares a voice over a megaphone. It's the kiosk attendant (who is, naturally, a salmon).

"Yeah, yeah," our salmon mutters as he paddles out to the far edge of the derby zone, delineated by orange floats bobbing on the slack tide at the extremity of the Millstone estuary, where the river empties into Newcastle Channel.

It is the first Sunday of September and a brilliant sunny morning. Away from the group, our salmon reaches into his tackle bag, takes out a houseplant mister, and spritzes his entire body with a 10:1 mixture of water and extra virgin olive oil. He then angles his body to the sun just so, causing his scales to flash and shimmy like a Vegas showgirl. (Salmon have kept the Vegas tradition alive in their tenure at the top of the food chain.)

So mesmerized is the sun by all this flashing and glinting from the planet's surface that she begins to descend for a closer look. Perhaps, at last, this is the mate the lovelorn sun has long been waiting for…

Soon the sun is hovering just a few feet above our salmon's kayak, which—being a two-seater—has a second cockpit behind the salmon, exposing the kayak's floor. With the sun directly overhead bathing the entire scene in her high-intensity lovelight, our salmon is able to look down into the second cockpit and gaze right through the polyetheylene resin hull of the kayak to observe the skeletons of humans, large and small, swimming in the sea below. Indeed, it's a DIY portable X-ray machine able to penetrate the ocean's murky depths beyond the unaided eye, like those colonels and generals who lined up on a New Mexico desert in the previous century to observe the first above-ground nuclear tests at Los Alamos. They closed their eyes, turned their backs to the blast, put their hands over their faces, and when the bomb went off, they could see the bones in their hands.

Whether these tests accelerated the planet's geomagnetic clock, we may never know. But what we do know is that every ten thousand years the North and South Poles reverse polarity in the time it takes to flick a tail. And with no small consequences. The previous reversal cost us Atlantis. And this most recent episode? As you can see, humans were tossed into the sea and salmon onto land. (The salmon have built some fantastic When-Humans-Roamed-the-Earth theme parks in the midwest to expand their range. Salmon are very enterprising and have taken to this landlubber thing quite well.)

Aided by the X-ray powers of the smitten sun, our clever salmon is able to reel in human after human, as large as they come. He tosses them into the hull through the second cockpit. And when that becomes too full, he fills the saddle bags slung over the kayak until he can carry no more. Then he winks at the sun, who starts to swoon just a little before taking a seat behind him in the second cockpit. And our salmon begins to paddle toward Newcastle Island in the harbour.

"You are out of bounds, sir! Please return your kayak immediately," squawks the megaphone in the distance.

"Take your stinkin' rules and shove 'em where the lice don't bite!" snorts the salmon.

Such manliness, the sun observes. And thoughful too! (For the sun knows how that epithet usually ends.)

The salmon commands the kayak forward toward Newcastle Island with confident, powerful strokes. They'll feast on barbecued human tonight and sleep on the beach. Then he'll knock together a simple smokehouse with whatever scraps of wood he finds lying around on the island and smoke the rest of the humans for long-term storage. The two of them could live on that all winter. He could build them a little cabana out of driftwood, hit up passing boaters for free martinis, a friendly poker game or two, trade smoked human for a bag of weed. And if they get cabin fever, he can sell the meat for cash and head to Vegas with his radiant lady luck.

The sun meanwhile is enthralled with the swift, masculine thrust of the kayak cleaving the water, delighting in the wind whipping through her corona and chromosphere, anticipating the climax of this wondrous union, bedazzled by the sequinned skin rippling and scintillating in the forward cockpit—each tiny scale a bursting, flooding, brimming world with no beginning and no end.

Who says dreams don't come true?

Backbone

My back is on a long journey
climbing a knotted rope anchored
to the cliff face with a right-between-the-eyelet
made of iron The eyelet is rust-pocked A fine
dusting of curry and chocolate drifts into
my cricket ball eyes as I ascend for I am the
folded wings resting
between my back's scapulae You could call it
a free ride (the crickets do) but there is always a price
to be paid I may be bat-blind from the dusting
but I will not go hungry into that
good knife-fight that awaits us all
I am meeting other creatures and anatomy
along the way The pigeon guillemots
nesting in small pants pockets on the cliff face
The cliff face is fully clad and there is pain
just a little but enough to send me to that
straw bed in the sheep manger I have carried
with me my whole life tucked under my
pleated wings The guillemots are deaf
and eye-plucked from the shelling
of the beach in the last war They do not see
my backbone or that they are ashore
and not at sea Their lips grow fat as kettle drums
Their beaks clack shut
then wide They perceive me in their
blindness as a pelagic invertebrate species
worthy of a meal My back will have to continue
its cliff face-off without me I always knew
it would end this way or some way
for nothing is too large to swallow whole
or too small to take five
and blow that sax to smithereens blow it

out the window out the door out your
asterisk out the tailpipe slathered with blueberry
enjambment and other tasty condiments blow it down
the entire Pacific flyway til you hit
Mexico

Postcards from the Electroplague

They say a watched pot never boils. But when no one was looking her pot of blood boiled over. And over. And over. Her red corpuscles rolled away, became stacks of poker chips at the roulette table. (She had been wealthy before the boiling incident.) The dealer spun the wheel with his he-man paw sheathed in a lineman's leather glove. Red-black-red-black-red-black-red-black-red-blackredblackredblackredblack ... The metal ball clickity-clacked around the wheel. She held her breath lest slight currents of warm air alter the ball's trajectory and final resting point. The ball was her compressed future. She longed to touch her stack of corpuscles once more for good luck. But it was against the rules.

*

The Earthworm Wars lasted ten months. During that period our planet, to put it bluntly, went to shit in a Sunday bonnet. The Earth experienced severe tachycardia when it no longer had the stabilizing influence of the worms carving out the correct frequencies as they wriggled their sinusoidal bodies through the crust. All the missing frequencies lay piled in hastily erected field hospitals and mass graves. Dirty bandages and makeshift splints were wrapped tight around their broken sine waves. The new frequencies that emerged (nature abhors a vacuum, and all that) resembled boa constrictors and pythons and legless crocodiles hanging from street lamps, lying coiled on rooftops, sliding down chimneys in the middle of the night. Now they say the Snake Wars are coming.

*

When the first aluminum child was born it was declared an abomination. A young mother breastfed her aluminum baby on Oprah while the zealots stood outside wailing in ancient tongues. When the mother took her aluminum baby to the neighbourhood park small dogs would growl and back away from the stroller. And when the child got old enough for school, it brought home a report card with straight A's. The other students were falling asleep at their desks and vomiting in school hallways bombarded with hidden messages pick-axing their porcelain craniums. Around this time kitchen foil began disappearing from supermarkets. Pallets in basements grew high with roll upon roll of the stuff.

Design

Within a week we all had learned how baby
octopi are born—a jelly flower's
petals burst one after next. Maybe
more than chaos came to build this bower

where I now sit, this garden lush
with pear and sage, feet naked on
the clover. Quaking body wants to hug
each flower like a lover. Five more dawns

and off I go to chemo-radiation.
Within the ancient texts we find the Torture
of the Phoenix (another Taoist machination)—
a tempering of steel and soul to gain a longer future.

And when my petals drop upon the earth
I hope to know not only night but birth.

And there we are

Looking back on it all, it is as though I was stranded aboard a shuttlepod trapped in a decaying orbit around a moribund planet without enough fuel or insight to achieve escape velocity. I pushed buttons, logged plot points, watered the arugula in the shipboard biodome as though the mission was still in progress, with a purpose that would mean something in the end. I ignored the approaching craters. So slow was their expansion, I could pretend I was simply in a holding pattern. And then you came aboard, teleported through the titanium hull. Or perhaps you were there all along, stowed away in the air-recycler. Or maybe you are the shuttlepod itself, my reality-husk handspun from prismatic filaments of my own hair. Whatever. You take control of the guidance system (which wouldn't be hard if you are, in fact, the shuttlepod) and alter the course heading.

It seems all wrong. We are going deeper in. I have no confidence. How can this ram-thrust toward disaster achieve a positive end? We struggle (for years, according to the ship's log) but not too fiercely, as it turns out. For beneath the churn and spew of river run, my dipper-faith (that pinfeather submarine in my breast) is quietly threading its way between the stones. The gyroscope gimbling below says this is a stable heading despite all optics to the contrary.

The pockmarked surface of the planet is about to swallow us. I close my eyes, brace for impact but feel only the skin on the back of my head wanting to peel away from my skull. I look up and see stars smashing toward us. You have somehow steered us off the crush at the last moment, parabolically arcing us back up toward an outer orbit, using the planet's own gravitational force, stretching it like a rubber band until it slingshots us off on a new trajectory with enough recoil that we can at last break free from the gravity trap of this damned planet (which turns out to be our salvation in the end, so there is some kind of a message here about suspending judgment or loving ourselves or being big enough to contain contradiction). And yes, we all saw that *Star Trek* episode. But that was the great thing about *Star Trek*—it was never really about outer space.

But wait. We are not done yet. Not while I'm still locked in this far-flung shuttlepod shooting etheric rapids, dodging howler fields and elephant swales, chasing this swelled mango of a universe begging to be split, known, named, tasted. And my shuttlepod has become a dull blade in the back, a whalebone corset, its own electric cliché dumbly blinking in a hydrogen haze of seven infant suns raggedy-dancing up a ridgeline at daybreak. It is all that stands between me and whatever-is-not-me. I want to touch something bigger than the buttons on my console. I was going to offer a clever contrivance at this point. Perhaps: "So I peel off the shuttlepod like a soiled sock, like a debutante's gown..." But this stiff husk is already gone, vanished as soon as I touched its rusted strands, heard the treefrog peeping from the mossy crust of rotted fencepost.

Yet somehow (and I do not remember doing this) I managed to take the shuttlepod's guidance system with me before the craft blinked out. (The guidance system would be the best of you, I suppose. Although you may really be me. But I still think of you as "you" when I miss you, which does not happen as often as it used to). I apparently folded it into a series of ever-smaller triangles as one might fold a flag when putting it to bed for the night. And this infinitely tiny wedge (for the folding will go on forever—it's a sort of Zeno's paradox) now seems to be contained in a small medicine pouch sewn from my own excess skin and strung around my neck, beneath my clothes, beneath my remaining skin, beneath my skeleton even. And there we are.

Depot

Sooner or later
we all enter the slumber-soot
lair of empty lolling dragons, their grey tongues pulsing
under greyer sky. They wait for us behind the Beer & Wine store.
They are not anxious. They know time is on their side.

They wait for us
to reach this long unwind of shallow gut
slung beneath our storefront certainty, complete with ticket window
built this morning by stage hands.

They wait for our forward campaign,
our echo-location through crumbling
subterranean switchbacks, past leprous walls. The ceaseless
flaking off, the buckled carpet stains rising up to meet us, the hardened
rat feces, the crematorium of hot-boxed butts, the sickly flickerflash
of some stuck dream with a bad ballast.

(This is not The Hero's Journey,
it's just the way to the bathroom.)

Until we arrive
at the Stations of the Cross—all fourteen of them
(although the eighth is locked), each with its own shrine and scriptures
for our meditation, our reconstruction, our linkage to an essence
beyond our withered slumping selves. Give us Gandhi, Shakespeare,
Betty Sue, our Holy Trinity of chrome-and-tile-clad prophecy.

We open our hairy bodies
to offer our sacraments through the city's
creaking sewers, through abraded neural tubes, through
kerosene-soaked backdoors askew on sagging hinges. The turbulence
of our evacuation rips paper-thin nests made from mud and
wasp spit off their fragile moorings in our brains, leaving our two
hemispheres pasted together with nothing but a thick rebellious buzzing.

We offer the best
of ourselves, and the worst, the loosing of fury
held too long, of the startled calf culled from the herd, of yearning
that splits the heart like a bivalve to reveal its bluish pearl.

We empty ourselves
into the swollen catacombs aflood with
all the discarded turtles and goldfish and priests from centuries past.

We empty ourselves
within the steel walls rising two-thirds of the way
to the acoustic ceiling tile heavens.

We empty ourselves
into the tenements and crack alleys and cherry-red
KitchenAid blenders, into uranium-tipped shells and Kevlar vests,
into asemic chemtrails chalking curdled skies, into NCIS episodes
we have seen seven times, into networked cloud storage, mutant
crops, gorged soccer stadiums, tin buckets of radioactive mopwater.

We empty ourselves
into the vacant lot at the end of my street
where she returned to unity one summer night while the neighbours
heard wild animal screams and cranked up their TVs.

We purge it all
into the dark void cleaving specificity
from surprise, our greasy matted psyches chasing a prayerbook
butterfly that lets us think we can maybe grow light enough
to lift off and start over again.

Outside,
upon the planet's toughened surface, a young mother
(just a girl herself) with unknown backstory and knee-high boots
pushes a black stroller across the rain-sluiced platform
to reach the last bus.

False Economy

It began, I now think, with the purpling leaves as the light fell. As my bare arms grew goosebumpy. As ravens and squirrels and tree frogs tucked into their evening roosts. As I scuffed my way through fir needle duff on my journey home. Or the illusion of home, since the true destination always remains a cipher until we arrive.

Es dunkelt I thought, although it had been thirty years since that German class in university. *Es dunkelt* rolled through my head like loose bolts in a tuna fish can. Loose bolts that must not be forgotten because they belong somewhere. Because they are waiting to reattach something important.

Leaves are not really purple. Except when *es dunkelt*. What are the true colours of the forest? If even hue is hostage to the vagaries of time-space, can anything be certain? And when did I lose my adaptation to sleep outdoors?

But we have a bigger problem. We are approaching the point in the story that is the actual beginning, and written in the way I had hoped to tell it all. The rest was just a confused preamble tacked on as an afterthought. And one that somehow managed to launch itself in the Modern Realist Tradition. Thus setting you up, I fear, to expect that you will learn more about me as we progress. We want stories about people after all, not unvetted ideas. Leave symbolism to the Surrealists, abstraction to the metaphysicians. Just load us up with nuanced personal detail to engage vicarious emotion and choke out any hatchlings of unbounded thought. Perhaps you have already started to form a theory about the true reason for my detour through the woods, or for taking German in university. Perhaps you are even imagining a gullible student's frothy affair with a German professor, a sexual act on a washing machine in a darkened laundry room at a faculty Christmas party at the Dean's home. At the very least, you must by now have formed an opinion on my gender. But none of this is relevant. There are larger concerns at stake.

My best advice is to view our bumpy start as a lesson in non-attachment and simply move forward unencumbered. I will try to make the transition as smooth as possible.

The forest was deeper and more perplexing than I had anticipated. I looked (as best I could in the *dunkelnden* light) for a place to bed down, some way to keep warm. I saw a fallow deer sleeping at the base of an ancient cedar. I lay beside it and pulled the deer's spots over myself. This worked very well, and the deer did not seem to notice. When I awoke the next morning, the deer was stiff and cold.

I said a brief blessing to the deer before leaving. I had heard (in university, perhaps) that certain Indigenous Peoples do this to creatures whose lives they take. All I could think of was: *es dunkelt*. But that felt sufficient. I reminded myself that the deer was, after all, an import from a foreign land, its ancestors having been shipped here in the previous century as a game species, born to die, to be of service. I privately thanked the genius who figured out how to make the value of a life rewritable. And to ambush any future insurgencies of conscience, I decided to compose a poem to the fallen deer whenever I finally arrived home.

I walked on, taking the spots with me. But by evening they were gone. I had spent them all on food and drink and some casual entertainment provided by a troupe of travelling clouds. So I found another deer. And another.

I did not notice when the last deer disappeared because by then I had enough spots to purchase all the garments and coordinating accessories and Cuisinart appliances I needed (plus some I didn't). I hired men to cut the forest (paying them in spots, of course) and then build me a large house (more of a city, really) to hold my various acquisitions. Each day when *es dunkelte*, I simply switched on the lights. Life had become much easier than during my forest period.

Although I was inland, I heard reports of the ocean (no longer contained by the trees) going berserk, leaping out of its bowl, its black skin pulling back for miles, leaving vast topographies of sea-bottom exposed. Due to these extreme low tides, marine rocks—clad in their thick pelage of green algae—were now on display. Roving horses mistook the rocks for pasture and bit down hard (essentially victims of unexamined habit and transgenerational neural networks), costing them their teeth. The horses were actually tarpans. And not the modern reconstruction of the species concocted by the Polish government in the nineteenth century. No, these were bonafide tarpans, long thought extinct. Without their teeth, these relict equines confronted the dialectics of survival: adapt or perish.

Their gut-smooth mouths became the undersides of gumboot chitons—pink, moist, yet surprisingly firm. The toothless tarpans befriended the enemy rocks before clamping down for good. The tarpans lay limp in the mud until the tide rolled in, lofting their coarse bodies skyward, each attached to its muck-sunk rock by a stalk of thick neck.

They had become—no, not seahorses. Pay attention. Expectation will undo you every time. You must re-invent yourself each moment if you seek authentic engagement with the universe. They were now sessile anemones, undulating beneath the waves, ensnaring other less adaptable species in their whippy legs. However when *es dunkelt*, they do become my night mares. (Why after all these years do I still recall *es dunkelt* but not the corresponding phrase for 'it grows bright'?)

Was I responsible for all this? The loss of the last known tarpans and trees and ex-pat fallow deer? The creation of sessile anemones? A spot-based monetary system? The great yawing of the sea? I had only wanted to stay warm. Time to boot up the laptop and compose another poem.

Barsby Park

1.

Wonder lies waiting,
twitching and flicking in muck,
gulping damp air beside the riverbank
at the base of rain-slicked wooden steps.
You never descend anymore because
of those forest people
slumbering in leaves, siphoning the cold nectar
from crumpled bags, compressing each stray galaxy
until it fits into bent shoes made
new—reborn by strapping duct tape to shrink the loose world
always sluicing in. Yet today is somehow
different, a beak busting through thin hull to taste the light.
Perhaps it is
the low pitch of this December sun
revealing the penciled-in boundary
between truth and dream, leading you deeper down
those warped planks not used since the age
of innocence. Everywhere all the seams are unravelling as you pass
indeterminate matrices
of naked
salmonberry and shapeless heaps draped in porous mesh
of golden leaves until you arrive at
the river's ever-slipping edge where you look down at your feet
to discover
a creature you have never seen. A dark scrawl pulsing in jelly sheath, waiting for you,
is there.

2.

Is there
a creature you have never seen? A dark scrawl pulsing in jelly sheath, waiting for you
to discover
the river's ever-slipping edge. Where you look down at your feet
of golden leaves until you arrive at
salmonberry and shapeless heaps draped in porous mesh
of naked
indeterminate matrices
of innocence everywhere. All the seams are unravelling as you pass
those warped planks not used since the age
between truth and dream. Leading you deeper down,
revealing the penciled-in boundary,
the low pitch of this December sun.
Perhaps it is
different—a beak busting through thin hull to taste the light
always sluicing in. Yet today is somehow
new. Reborn by strapping duct tape to shrink the loose world
until it fits into bent shoes made
from crumpled bags. Compressing each stray galaxy
slumbering in leaves, siphoning the cold nectar
of those forest people.
You never descend anymore because
at the base of rain-slicked wooden steps,
gulping damp air beside the riverbank,
twitching and flicking in muck,
wonder lies waiting.

What remains

At the end of Maki Road, beyond the Living Forest
campground, lies a tomb of ghosts and statues
from a civilization past. I can hear them whispering

among the broom and brambles and estuary
grasses. Some days I think I understand
their language, the meaning of a stairway

up a coal slag going nowhere. Or the giant
iron spool thirty feet tall. Deeper in the forest
the fractured concrete walls of an old building

with more forest growing inside, roof long gone.
I step over the doorsill, walk across the soft
earthen floor strewn with fir cones to reach the small

window with its view of furrowed trunks. A brown
creeper needles its way up the bark in front of me. Somewhere
nearby a crow strikes up a conversation as persistent

as the moss devouring the walls. I cannot tell
if its raspy call is coming from the forest inside
or the forest without.

Armadillo

Once there were two brothers who lived on the back of an armadillo. The armadillo was so large and slow-moving that the two brothers, along with everyone else aboard the lumbering beast, assumed it was a planet.

As children, the two brothers were great inventors. When they were ten, they made a waterwheel from their mother's teaspoons. The family stirred its tea with butter knives after that. The waterwheel powered a small defibrillator the brothers had built from an electric shaver. Their father grew a beard after that. The brothers searched high and low and in every corner of their yard, and even the neighbour's yard, looking for something to defibrillate. But they could find nothing fibrillating. This was a setback to their research. They put their homemade defibrillator and waterwheel away.

When the brothers grew up, their careers took them to opposite ends of the armadillo (which they still thought to be a planet). One brother inserted sonic probes deep into the creature to record the ultra low-frequency rumblings. These rumblings were actually the armadillo's heart beating. The other brother constructed an enormous saucer-shaped ear and pointed it heavenward to record the faint strands of star chatter hidden among space noise. These chattering songs were, in fact, mating vocalizations of amorous armadillos a great distance away.

The brothers, being full-fledged scientists by now, knew all about beat frequencies: the sonic outcome when one frequency is laid atop another. And so they combined their recordings of inner and outer space to see what would happen. The resulting pulse triggered ancient neural pathways, flooding the two brothers with a cascade of endorphins and euphoria (to say nothing of its affect on the armadillo). It was at this point that the corporate sector took an interest in the brothers' research.

Amplifiers were erected across the land so the beats would reach the entire population. Soon people were standing in line all night to purchase the latest release of neck-collar receivers. A free pad of post-it notes accompanied each receiver since quite a lot was being forgotten by now. (Hypomnesia turned out to be an unanticipated consequence of the addiction to beats.)

Things could have gone on this way indefinitely, or at least until all available surfaces were filled with post-it notes. However, the armadillo began to fibrillate. Cans fell from shelves. Fruit fell from trees. Birds fell from perches. Committees were struck to assess the Falling Crisis. Emergency Response Teams were deployed to all corners of the armadillo, although most forgot their mission and wandered aimlessly from town to town, opening pop-up road-kill cafés and sleeping in barns.

The two brothers managed to revive each other from their euphoric drift. They sensed they bore some responsibility for the current predicament. They vaguely recalled something about a defibrillator. The brothers returned to their childhood home where they searched high and low and in every corner of their yard, and even the neighbour's yard, looking for something they dimly remembered building many years ago. But the longer they searched, the hazier their compromised memories grew until they thought they were looking for a Christmas fruitcake.

Their parents, who no longer recalled they had two sons, believed the brothers were workmen come to replace the roof tiles. After a few hours, the elderly couple offered the workmen tea with butter knives. Eventually, the armadillo expired and the falling stopped.

Field Notes from Tonal Outposts

We will swing iron weights from silk cords tied
to our scrotum. We will up the load daily.

> She was touched by the contagion of his exquisitely sculpted
> mind.

We will beat our arms and legs with a sock stuffed with
rocks and sewn shut, which you will make.

> She stepped out of her newspaper skin, watched the language
> fall from her body in brittle pieces, petalling the ground.

We will increase the stone size weekly starting with aquarium
gravel then driveway chip then river rock.

> Her raw viscera wandered back alleys littered
> with hieroglyphics she could neither read nor write.

We will wield our sock hammer correctly to drive vacancy
from our moon-washed bones until our limbs become steel rods.

> She saw divinity gutted upon the puddled firmament
> star-shot by dirty halos on spent condoms.

We will lean with all our weight on a thick bamboo pole sunk into
the tender gulley of our windpipe.

> Every ten thousand years a planet's magnetic terminals reverse their
> polarity in the time it takes an unmoored eyelash to land on a cheek.

We will bear the brunt. We will exchange pole for spear
after one month.

> When the world drops away like stage walls, is it love
> or a nervous breakdown?

We will lie on the floor and have you stand on our
skull to release the cranial sutures that ossified after birth.

Those who manifest stigmata always bleed from the palms
although Christ was nailed through the wrists.

We will take half your weight tonight, and all
tomorrow.

Slowly the fiddlehead of her brainstem unfurled and sprouted
cordate leaves that overflying words would perch upon.

We will sleep on a wooden floor with a one-by-two plank
beneath our spine.

She folded herself into an accordion book to hold
his story.

We will reserve our hardness for our mission. We will straw-feed
on your yearning.

New Apostolic Church imploring her nightly to be reborn
as New Alcoholic Church. Temptation is everywhere.

We will recycle our urine and semen
but not our feces.

She watched a garter snake consume a field mouse
over an hour, hind foot twitching 'til the last.

We will harness brute oxen to the watercart and turn the wheel
in the rejuvenating direction, reversing the vector of time.

She scrawled the doctrine of his alchemy
along an underpass wall where the sand people slept.

We will become a corpse-free Immortal leaving no heirs. Our only issue:
your field notes from these tonal outposts along our celestial body.

Deluge

Rain does sluice the cobblestones
of lust and promises and shoes
The young wash past in oily foam
as rain does sluice the cobblestones
Next the tin can altar comes
then the pallets turned to pews
Rain does sluice the cobblestones
of lust and promises and shoes

The Patient

Every morning she swallowed three pills
with a glass of water while sitting up in bed. Every Monday
she walked into a clinic where they extracted three
teaspoons of blood into slender tubes. Her blood was the colour
of pomegranate guts, of a woodpecker's bright crest plunging
through pine-scented forest. Sometimes
she would wait in a room with other faces until she heard
her name. At the end of each clinic day she would stare at a
backlit screen at home and watch numbers swim
past. The numbers were free-floating in her blood
like tadpoles newly burst from their jellied egg mass.
They were also free-floating on her screen thanks to the dark art
of information theory and transport.

It was all very abstract. Until the morning she swallowed
three numbers with a glass of pomegranate guts while sitting
in a backlit forest. Faces swam past in slender tubes. She ate eggs
with jelly straight off the teaspoon as she waited to be
transported through the dark arts. Information is
made of glass. Should it plunge into your free-floating
home it can never be extracted. But you will know the scent of blood
the colour of pine, the brightness of water, the clinical difference
between a woodpecker's stare and a burst
screen. In a room of abstractions
every theory wears a pillbox hat. She took her bed for a walk.
At the end she heard three tadpoles call her name.

Crown of Thorns

the sperm of
jesus christ is believed to be
a snail

a hermaphrodite
will swoop and dive in unison
by certain schools of devout christians

the snails sex life
as well as some atheists
is unbelievably complicated to start with

the evidence offered includes
they are hermaphrodites each possessing a vagina and
the virgin birth since high school biology

two penises
tells us this can only lead to
mating

two X chromosomes
can take up to twelve hours
the position is further supported by much
which is understandable

early medieval art depicting
the foreplay involves firing
jesus as a woman
solid (and often lethal)
complete with breasts suggesting
darts

the true reason they all came
into each others bodies:
to behold

* * *

Assembled by interlacing photo captions from a
microbiology textbook with a blog about Jesus.

Urban Grammar

To wander the city at midnight. To punctuate
its unlit sentences, its tumbledown ruck. Ammonia
caresses, fetid guzzle, flash of headlight on dark

trickle—a stuck zipper, sticky with caved-in
imagination. This soft gush of rotted meaning face down
on the sewer grate. One sentence away

a bucket of narrative strands. Writhing. Balling and unballing.
Coughing up loose flecks of identity. Awaiting the right
mark. In the right place. To give shape to abandoned

avenues of thought, to alleys gutted by
dog's bark. The frantic bury of shadow, a locket ripped
from a neck as souvenir, a stream of hot piss

coursing down street. Bristling with packs of wild
commas, snarl of ellipsis, an apostrophe's glowing eyes.
These are the necessary notes to signify

the heart paused, the door ajar, the possessive case
of a padlocked dumpster, the rattle of chain, the exclamation of
foghorn, the full stop of the boxcar, the slam-shut

hatch (it is the pauses that assign meaning, yield story, withoutthemwearelost
this is the business of myth-making—each night on shaling skin
a new creation theory is born)

Show me the fetal-curled question mark
slumbering beneath the steps, pale larva glued to wool
blanket. The cyclone of newspapers spiraling

through the underpass, the dangling promise, the run-on
string of phonemes tunneling into the sand to hide behind a wall
of spawning salmon, the slurry of fists

their hard landing, all the split infinitives, the compound
eternities, passive voids, speech bubbles burst, spew of
sentient fragments, the orphaned

                  lines, indented dreams. Let me feel the urgent press

of chisel-tip sharpie on switch box, the hiss of paint bomb
the gouge of penknife on pole, the icy punch
of adrenaline against my skull, the need to punctuate

the night, to sensify
to stuff the hole, duck the sirens. To leave the right mark
in the right place. To sort all the vipers and

fill all the fire escapes with stars. Let me weave the littered
gastric streets into a scabrous arm mainlined with dopamine and
dirty speedballs to score the symphony

of existence on these listing exoskeletons—grey as desiccated
brains softly whiffling in their sleep, dreaming of I-beam legs
and tarpaper wings, their prodigal return to prehistory

when cities roamed free, ecstatic rebar frames skimming froth
and swale, roosting on crags, commandeering hot thermals
to loft them toward the sun, swell of cauldron and

lung, rising vast through a blue breath not yet exhaled.

carbon leakage

when a half moon hangs in the mid-morning sky
when a rainforest ignites
when a crowd of butterflies applauds a waterfall
when the skin of a planet is worn on a body stuffed with straw
when crabs scuttling across a tidepool are a video animation
when smoke takes on a shape and aims a taser
when sea gooseberries wash ashore and recapitulate the constellations
when scientists thaw a Siberian virus from the permafrost
when an eagle-cam atop a fir records a murder
when a father pushes a stroller beneath ash-laden sky
when apocalypse and miracle arrive on the same train

Garden

Deep in the garden lush and wild
Beneath a rotting log
A salamander grows three eyes
Deep in the garden lush and wild
You love each tumour like a child
An owl gives birth to rolling fog
Deep in the garden lush and wild
Beneath a rotting log

Shortly before the end

Shortly before the end, their minds turned sleek and black and were last seen bobbing and diving among small, open fishboats in the harbour. The golden light scattered diamonds atop the sea whenever a lean mind broke the surface. Each mind had a tight band around its neck and a string on one leg. This allowed it to continue searching and biting down on anything slippery it might encounter while scouring the murky depths. The collar prevented the mind from assimilating its catch, thus rendering each mind into an immaculate self-propelled satchel that was relieved of its still squirming bounty by a higher power every time it bobbed to the surface and the string was reeled in. By afternoon, the collars were removed and the ravenous minds were allowed to eat just enough of their haul to remain conscious and nourish brain cells. Then they were shut away in wicker crates until the following day.

Codex Exterminarius

eelgrass rock me in your sonatA=Tempo arms, shield my translucent
body with your soft rabbiT=Avalanche, hide the twisted
concrete upwell of each civiC=Galaxy from my bowling ball eyes
just a little while longer, let's join a touareG=Caravan in the sahara
you can be my piloT=Astro guide into the mysteries
above while we escorT=Armada of pulsing moon jellies across
stranded skies until they exhale a novA=Tracer to light our journey
home, teach me your cobalT=Axiom, your throat sung
equation to wake the cobrA=Tempest that will hurl us
back to that thundering mustanG=Century drenched in hoofbeats and
whipsheet manes, tails, lariaT=Allure (I can feel their hot breath
on my gelatinous skin, lofting me atop a sequoiA=Titan) this sharp loss
of altitude, I watch a luminA=Thunderbird archangel dim while
wisps of cloud (the spiriT=Avenger) escape from its pale nostrils—
whose sickly plunge into this crownviC=Genesis moss trough is next?
goshawk rock me in your omegA=Talon grip, shield my translucent body

until the end

* * *

*a mapping of our cultural genome in an age of post-peak oil, where the Adenine-
Thymine and Cytosine-Guanine base-pair couplings are constructed from cars*

Star Wars

It was a night like every other for the skyful of stars. They twinkled merrily, light of heart and mind, with nary a care in their pretty little stellar gases. Things had been going on this way since eternity (or possibly just 13.7 billion years, depending on whom you ask) without a hint of petty jealousies over who was the brightest or best positioned. This equanimity was possible because each star abided by a solipsistic worldview, believing it alone existed while all others were mere projections (astral projections, if you like) of its consciousness.

But on this particular night, a line of enquiry was cast into the celestial pool. An insignificant star in the lower right quadrant (not even assigned a constellation) winked out the following question through a series of solar flares: How do you know that you are the real one and not a projection?

The heavens grew uncustomarily quiet. The stars blinked. Having posed the question, our Philosopher Star set off across the universe on a solitary search for meaning (as Philosopher Stars are wont to do) and was never seen again.

A great deal of flickering ensued until the firmament was in such a self-doubting tizzy, it scarcely knew which way to rotate. This confusion left the stars vulnerable to exploitation by less scrupulous types. New stars emerged, peddling Truth for $18.95 in paperback. Those with the best marketing plans soon each had a small flock of stars traipsing across the sky behind them. One particularly savvy Truth peddler (who was up on Spacebook before the others were even thinking about it) drew a vast following now known as the Milky Way. Flocks grew into empires, wars were fought, age-old stellar relations were ripped asunder.

The astronomic tumult soon tangled the guy wires for the Entire Known Realm. Birds plunged into mountains, planes into skyscrapers, sailors drank the sea, planets seared, orbits wobbled, electrons could not decide if they were particle or wave. The stars meanwhile, having long since forgotten the instigating question, popped like kernels in hot oil, each offering up the mystery of its innards as it raced to be the biggest in the coming white-out.

Acknowledgements

Some of the writing in this collection was made possible by a grant from the British Columbia Arts Council, for which I am grateful.

Many of the pieces in this collection first appeared in one of the following magazines or anthologies. My thanks to these editors and publishers for supporting my work.

Big Smoke Poetry
The Cabinet of Heed
The Capilano Review
Cascadia Review
Dark Mountain
Epizootics!
EVENT
Front
Lake Journal
Literary Review of Canada
The New Quarterly
OJAL (Open: Journal of Arts & Letters)
Poetry Is Dead
Prairie Fire
Riddle Fence
Ryga
subTerrain
Uneven Earth
Watershed Sentinel
Zahir Tales

Another Dysfunctional Cancer Poem Anthology (Mansfield Press, 2018)

Cascadia (Leaf Press, 2015)

Igniting the Green Fuse: Four Canadian Women Poets (Above & Beyond Productions, 2012)

Make It True: Poetry from Cascadia (Leaf Press, 2015)

Multiverse: an international anthology of science fiction poetry (Shoreline of Infinity, 2018)

Refuse: CanLit in Ruins (Book*hug, 2018)

Tesseracts Eleven (Edge Science Fiction and Fantasy Publishing, 2007)

About the Author

Kim Goldberg is the author of eight books of poetry and nonfiction. Her quirky, reality-bending poems and fables have appeared in numerous magazines and anthologies in North America and abroad. Her first poetry collection, *Ride Backwards on Dragon*, was shortlisted for the Gerald Lampert Memorial Award. Her *Red Zone* collection of poems about urban homelessness has been taught in university literature courses. Kim holds a degree in biology and is an avid birdwatcher and field naturalist. Before turning to poetry, she was a freelance journalist covering environmental issues. Originally from Oregon, Kim and her family came to Canada in the 1970s as Vietnam War resisters. She lives in Nanaimo, British Columbia.

Other Books by Kim Goldberg

Undetectable (Pig Squash Press, 2016)

Red Zone (Pig Squash Press, 2009)

Ride Backwards on Dragon (Leaf Press, 2007)

Where to See Wildlife on Vancouver Island (Harbour Publishing, 1997)

Vox Populi (New Star Books, 1993)

Submarine Dead Ahead! (Harbour Publishing, 1991)

The Barefoot Channel (New Star Books, 1990)